DonaldShaw.org

PRESENTS...

Published by Lena Shaw

www.DonaldShaw.org

Ebook edition created 2018

ISBN-10: 1984042602

ISBN-13: 978-1984042606

Disclaimer: All facts in this book were gained from common and reputable sources in print and on the internet. The book benefits from international fair use provisions set aside in law. The author is grateful to J.K. Rowling for creating the amazing world of Harry Potter which has allowed this book to be written. If any detail within this title is found to be incorrect, the author will be happy to publish a correct version.

TABLE OF CONTENTS

THE ULTIMATE 500 HARRY POTTER FACTS EVERY FAN SHOULD KNOW

Harry Potter is the phenomenon that has swept the globe, smashing records and nesting in all of our hearts. Yes, it's almost unbelievable to understand how all of it had happened and why the world fell in love with the boy wizard. From the fantastic books written by the British author J.K. Rowling to the blockbuster movies that were welcomed by hundreds of fans outside the cinemas worldwide, Harry Potter's legacy lives on and is still felt in the pop culture.

That's why we'll look at the ultimate list of 500 (yeah, you read that right) Potter-related facts! Enjoy and prepare to be knocked off your brooms!

HARRY POTTER BOOKS FACTS

The seven Harry Potter books have become instant classics and something no child should grow up without. So, here are some of the most captivating facts about the books…

1. *Harry Potter and the Philosopher's Stone* was originally published on 26th June 1997.

---

2. The Harry Potter books in the United Kingdom have been published by Bloomsbury whereas in the United States by Scholastic.

---

3. Only 500 copies of *Harry Potter and the Philosopher's Stone* were initially published by Bloomsbury.

---

4. The first Harry Potter book has different titles in the UK and the US – in the UK it's called *Harry Potter and the Philosopher's Stone* and in the States it's known as *Harry Potter and the Sorcerer's Stone*. Hmm, interesting, right?

---

5. Picture this – in case you take every sold copy of Harry Potter ever and order it from one end to the other of the Earth, the books would circle the equator more than 1.6 times! Wow!

---

6. The fifth book in the series, *Harry Potter and the Order of the Phoenix*, was sold in over 5 million copies, and wait for it, in just the first 24 HOURS of its release! Mind-blowing!

---

7. Its sequel, *Harry Potter and the Half-Blood Prince*, broke the record with eleven million sold books in one day.

---

8. *Harry Potter and the Deathly Hallows*, the last book in the series, topped them with 15 million copies purchased around the globe.

---

9. The motto of the wizarding school Hogwarts is 'Draco Dormiens Nunquam Titillandus' which can be translated into 'Never tickle a sleeping dragon'.

---

10. The total number of words in the Harry Potter book series is 1,100,086.

---

11. The books have been published in around 200 countries.

---

12. You can find the Harry Potter books in more than 79 languages.

---

13. Some of these languages include old ones like Ancient Greek and Latin.

---

14. What's interesting is that the names of the Hogwarts houses are also translated.

---

15. The novels were the first books meant for children to be featured on the New York Time's bestseller list since 1952 when *Charlotte's Web* by E.B. White found its place there as well.

---

16. The English version of *Harry Potter and the Order of the Phoenix* was the only book written in English to top the bestseller lists in France.

---

17. The first book was rejected by publishers many times before Bloomsbury eventually took it in 1996.

18. The Coca-Cola Company got the rights to tie in their products with the release of the first Harry Potter book under one condition by the author.

19. The condition was that they should donate a huge sum of money to the Reading Is Fundamental initiative that encourages children to pick up books and read in the USA.

20. Numbers are very important in the series. For instance, the number 3 is found in the trio of main characters, Harry defeating the basilisk in the third stab, Hagrid knocking three times on Hogwarts's front door.

21. The number 7 is also HUGE in the series. Students study 7 years at Hogwarts, there are 7 Harry Potter books, 7 players on a Quidditch team, 7 classes at Hogwarts, 7 Weasley children, and so on.

---

22. As one of the most buzzed about books ever, *Harry Potter and the Deathly Hallows* was given code names by the publishers to stop leaks.

---

23. The seventh book ends with the sentence, “All was well.”

---

24. The last book is also dedicated to the fans. “...and to you, if you have stuck with Harry until the very end,” Rowling writes.

---

25. The first Harry Potter book begins with the sentence, “Mr. and Mrs. Dursley, of number four Privet Drive, were proud to say that they were perfectly normal, thank you very much.”

---

26. The first year at Hogwarts actually takes place in 1991.

27. The Platform 9 ¾ actually exists on the real King's Cross Station in London. The platform was erected as a sign of respect towards Harry Potter's legacy and serves as one of the main attractions for fans from all over the world.

---

28. According to the books, Hogwarts is situated in Scotland.

---

29. Before the eyes of a muggle, it appears as an old ruin thanks to many charms.

---

30. Hogwarts was founded by Godric Gryffindor, Salazar Slytherin, Helga Hufflepuff, and Rowena Ravenclaw.

---

31. It was in the year 990 AD.

32. Salazar Slytherin built the Chamber of Secrets.

33. The crests of the Hogwarts houses contain their signature animals – a lion for Gryffindor, a serpent for Slytherin, a badger for Hufflepuff, and a raven for Ravenclaw.

34. Each house has a corresponding element – Gryffindor represents fire, Slytherin represents water, Ravenclaw is associated with air, whereas Hufflepuff with earth.

35. A, B, C, D, and F are so overrated, right? At Hogwarts the grades you can receive include Outstanding, Exceeding Expectations, and Acceptable. But you wouldn't want to get Poor, Dreadful nor Troll because that would mean that you failed :(

36. Besides the original seven books, J.K. Rowling wrote 3 companion books (to the delight of fans). They're textbooks known as *The Tales of Beedle the Bard*, *Fantastic Beasts and Where to Find Them*, and *Quidditch Through the Ages*.

---

37. For charity purposes, Jo wrote a Harry Potter prequel story of around 800 words.

---

38. It's a short story in which the main characters are James Potter and Sirius Black.

---

39. The story was written on a card and was sold at an auction for 25,000 pounds.

---

40. Sadly, in 2017 the card was stolen from the owner.

---

41. The name Harry Potter got 29 mentions in the main text of the first book, whereas Voldemort 38.

---

42. The character Harry Potter doesn't speak until the second chapter of *Harry Potter and the Philosopher's Stone*.

---

43. His first word is 'nearly'.

---

44. Even though it's all about the school of magic and spells, only 4 incantations make an appearance in the first book.

---

45. They are Wingardium Leviosa, Alohomora, Petrificus Totalus, and Locomotor Mortis.

---

46. The fourth book in the series *Harry Potter and the Goblet of Fire* could have been called *Harry Potter and the Doomspell Tournament*. Personally, I'm glad it isn't called that.

---

47. I don't know about you, but many readers of the books struggled with the pronunciation of Hermione.

---

48. So, to clarify this, Jo Rowling wrote a special scene where Hermione explains how her name is pronounced to Viktor Krum.

---

49. The last Harry Potter book was supposed to end with 'scar'. But after she finished writing it, Jo decided to put 'All was well' instead.

---

50. Originally, Arthur Weasley was planned to die in *Harry Potter and the Order of the Phoenix*. But Jo replaced him with Sirius.

---

51. The story of the Deathly Hallows was inspired by Geoffrey Chaucer's *The Pardoner's Tale*.

---

52. Some of the alternative titles for *Harry Potter and the Deathly Hallows* were *Harry Potter and the Elder Wand* or *Harry Potter and the Peverell Quest*, which Jo thought was corny and immediately removed it. Agreed!

---

53. All the criminals in the wizarding world are imprisoned in Azkaban – a dreadful place guarded by the even more dreadful Dementors. Grrr!

---

54. The wizarding world of the Harry Potter books has a couple of media outlets including the daily newspaper called The Daily Prophet and the magazine Quibbler.

---

55. Sport is a huge deal in the wizarding world, too, you know. Wizards play Quidditch – a sport the author invented herself.

---

56. She later spoke in an interview that she came up with the sport after an argument with her then-boyfriend.

---

57. Quidditch has 700 fouls.

---

58. Americans have an alternative sport called Quodpot. And we want tickets for this awesome game!!!

---

59. After the release of all the seven books, J.K. Rowling launched the website Pottermore in 2012.

60. Pottermore is a news company which offers a unique experience and details connected to the books and the wizarding world of Harry.

61. It features unique tests designed by J.K. Rowling like the Sorting Hat Quiz and Discover Your Patronus Quiz.

62. Besides that, Rowling wrote exclusive, never-before-seen material connected to the backstories of the main characters and other new aspects of the world.

63. In 2016, J.K. Rowling collaborated with Jack Thorne and John Tiffany to create *Harry Potter and the Cursed Child* – a two-part play.

64. The play debuted on West End to raving reviews and now it moved even to Broadway in New York.

---

65. The script of the play, which is based on Rowling's story, was released to the public on 31st July and it became an instant bestseller

---

66. The Cursed Child play gained a lot of attention because of another reason as well. Hermione was played by an actress of color – Noma Dumezweni.

---

67. Rowling released a series of 3 eBooks called Pottermore Presents, which gather all exclusive information from the site in one place.

---

68. The individual titles of these 3 eBooks are – *Short Stories from Hogwarts of Heroism, Hardship and Dangerous Hobbies*, *Short Stories from Hogwarts of Power, Politics and Pesky Poltergeists*, and *Hogwarts: An Incomplete and Unreliable Guide*.

---

69. Rowling relied upon the Latin language to invent the spells such as Expelliarmus and Incendio.

---

70. The Harry Potter books are favorite among famous stars as well. Some of the celebrities publicly sharing their love for Harry Potter include the master of horror – Stephen King, the actors – Lily Collins and Ezra Miller, the singer – Shawn Mendes and many more.

---

71. Stephen King also said that Dolores Umbridge makes a perfect villain comparing her even to Hannibal Lecter.

---

72. Rowling explained that Dumbledore could sometimes see Harry under the Invisibility Cloak thanks to his ability to perform magic without saying the spells out loud.

---

73. The spell he used for that is called 'Homenum Revelio'.

---

74. When Arthur Weasley goes into the phone booth, he dials 62442 to go to the Ministry.

---

75. On a normal telephone keypad, these numbers give the word 'magic'.

---

76. The Dark Mark on the Death Eaters' arms in the end faded into a scar.

---

77. It's a common practice for children with magical abilities to be tutored at home until they reach their eleventh year. A perfect example of that are the Weasleys.

---

78. All the fractioned platforms at King's Cross actually serve witches and wizards.

---

79. The maximum number of O.W.Ls. (Ordinary Wizarding Levels) a wizard can take is 12.

---

80. Garden gnomes are regarded as pests by wizards. Why? They eat roots of plants and make holes in the earth.

---

81. Only people who have seen someone die can see the magical creatures called thestrals. And Harry can see them in the fifth book after experiencing Cedric's death.

82. The pictures in the wizarding world can move thanks to a potion. Shut up and take our money, because we need that more than anything!

83. We all know that the powerful Amortentia potion smells of the person we love most. And the third scent Hermione picks up is really Ron's hair.

84. There are around three thousand wizards in the United Kingdom.

85. There are ten known pure-bred species dragons in the wizarding world.

86. The members of the Order of the Phoenix communicated through their patronuses.

87. The wizarding money comes only in coins, not bills.

88. There are 3 types of coins in the wizarding world – golden Galleons, silver Sickles, and bronze Knuts.

89. A Sickle equals 29 Knuts.

90. One Galleon equals 17 Sickles.

91. If you're wondering how much that would be in Muggle money – one galleon is worth around 5 pounds.

92. Magic can't bring dead people back to life.

93. When a child is born in the wizarding world, a magical quill detects that and writes it in a book.

94. There are, however, children who have magical parents but don't have magic themselves. These children are called squibs.

95. One famous squib is Argus Filch – the caretaker at Hogwarts.

96. There are numerous uses of a dragon blood. One of them is – oven cleaner! Can you believe that?

97. The inscription on the Mirror of Erised is written in Latin and when translated it means “I show not your face but your heart’s desire.”

98. The epilogue in the final book takes place in 2017.

99. 31st October 1991 is a very important date because it’s the day when it’s generally accepted that Harry, Ron, and Hermione became friends. On that day, they defeated the troll in the girls’ bathroom.

100. Harry’s parents were murdered on Halloween.

101. There are 11 respected and long-established wizarding schools around the world.

---

102. Their registration is with the International Confederation of Wizards.

---

103. Ilvermorny is the American version of Hogwarts.

---

104. Some of the other famous wizarding schools are Beauxbatons Academy of Magic in France, Castelobruxo in Brazil, Durmstrang Institute in Northern Europe, Mahoutokoro in Japan, Uagadou in Africa.

---

105. The only curse word to appear in all seven books is 'bitch'.

---

106. It's said by Molly Weasley just before she kills Bellatrix Lestrange in the last book.

107. Rowling considered killing Ron but opted out of it. We can't be gladder!

108. Boggart is a shape-shifting type of creature that takes the form of the fear of a person.

109. Like poltergeists, the boggart isn't alive.

110. One of the ways to defeat it is the spell 'Riddikulus' as can be seen in the third book.

111. In one of the early notes, Rowling referred to the subject Herbology as 'Herbalism'.

112. Some of the mandatory subjects in the first year from these early stages include Alchemy, Divination, and Beasts. The situation was different in the final draft.

113. There are around twenty known ghosts at Hogwarts.

114. Each has its own ghost: Gryffindor has Nearly Headless Nick, Slytherin has Bloody Baron, Ravenclaw has Helena Ravenclaw, and Hufflepuff has the Fat Friar.

115. The ghost Nearly Headless Nick's full name is Sir Nicholas De Mimsy-Porpington and he was close to a king.

116. He was almost beheaded, but the job wasn't done well, thus gaining his nickname.

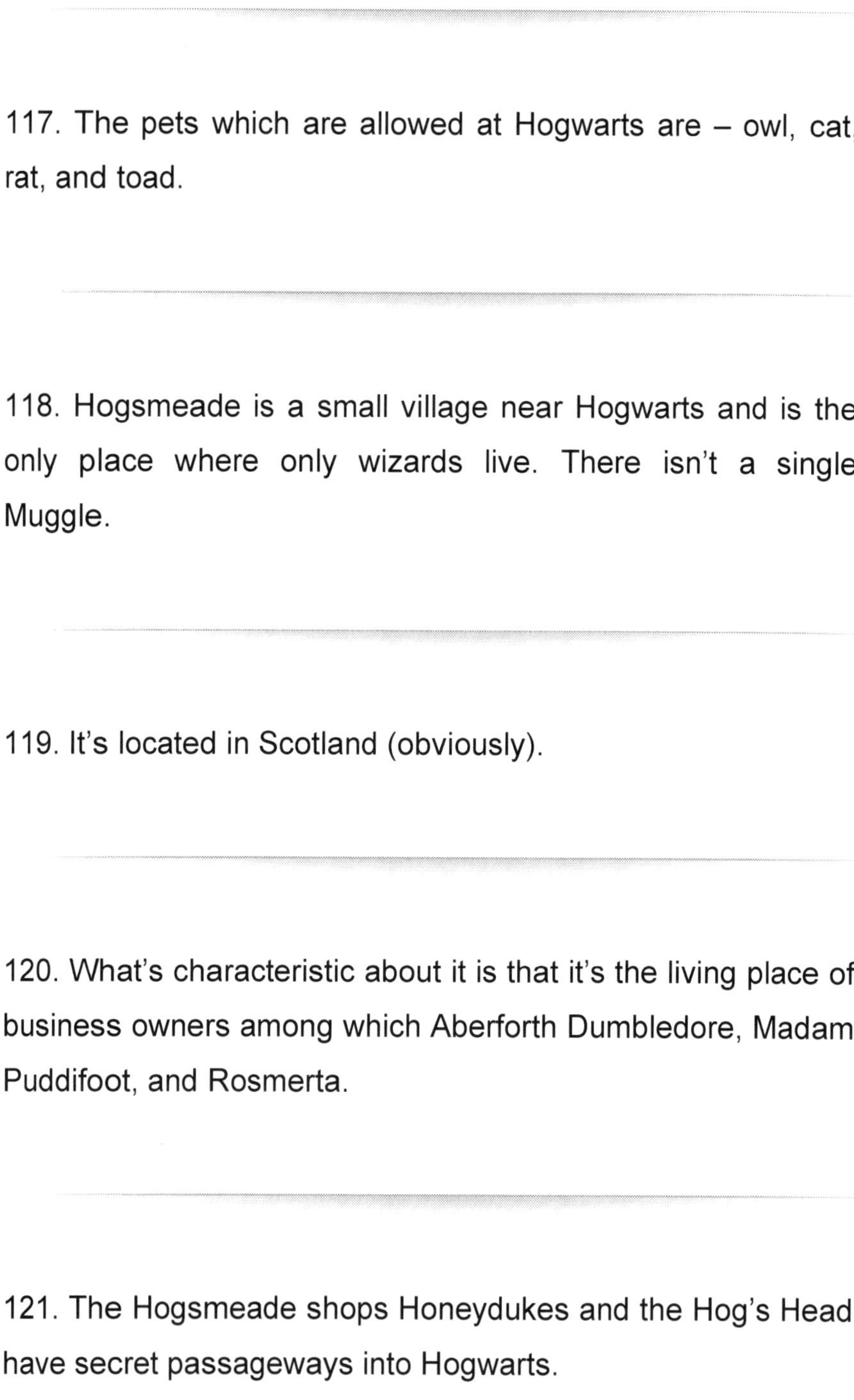

117. The pets which are allowed at Hogwarts are – owl, cat, rat, and toad.

118. Hogsmeade is a small village near Hogwarts and is the only place where only wizards live. There isn't a single Muggle.

119. It's located in Scotland (obviously).

120. What's characteristic about it is that it's the living place of business owners among which Aberforth Dumbledore, Madam Puddifoot, and Rosmerta.

121. The Hogsmeade shops Honeydukes and the Hog's Head have secret passageways into Hogwarts.

122. Butterbeer is one of the most popular beverages in the wizarding world and it tastes a bit like butterscotch.

123. It's worth 2 Sickles and Hogwarts students often buy it in Hogsmeade.

124. Despite Butterbeer, some of the other most popular beverages include firewhiskey, brandy, gin, mead, chocolate liqueur, and others.

125. Rowling went so far into the creation of her universe to invent new meals and foods. One such example is Celia Barnett's Supasnacks.

126. You'd be surprised to find out that the food at Hogwarts is much like what we eat as well – bacon, steak, porridge, pumpkin, beef, stew, potatoes, and so on.

---

127. Music is very important in the wizarding world. There's even an extracurricular subject at Hogwarts.

---

128. Weird Sisters is one famous band that young wizards love to listen to.

---

129. The Wizarding Wireless Network is a place where wizards embrace culture. Just like a streaming service.

---

130. Inside the Elder Wand, there's a Thestral hair.

---

131. Back to history, Azkaban wasn't always a prison. In the past, it was a fortress occupied by the Dark Wizard Ekrizdis, who captured Muggle sailors and tortured them there. Sounds even spookier than the Dementors.

---

132. Everyone's favorite half-giant can't conjure a Patronus. So sad for him.

---

133. Proud to be Hufflepuff? Good for you. Hufflepuff won the House Cup in 2015.

---

134. Hogwarts's permanent residents are the students, the ghosts, staff, and Peeves.

---

135. There are multiple subjects that students learn over the course of their seven years at Hogwarts. Transfiguration, Charms, Defense Against the Dark Arts, Potions, Astronomy,

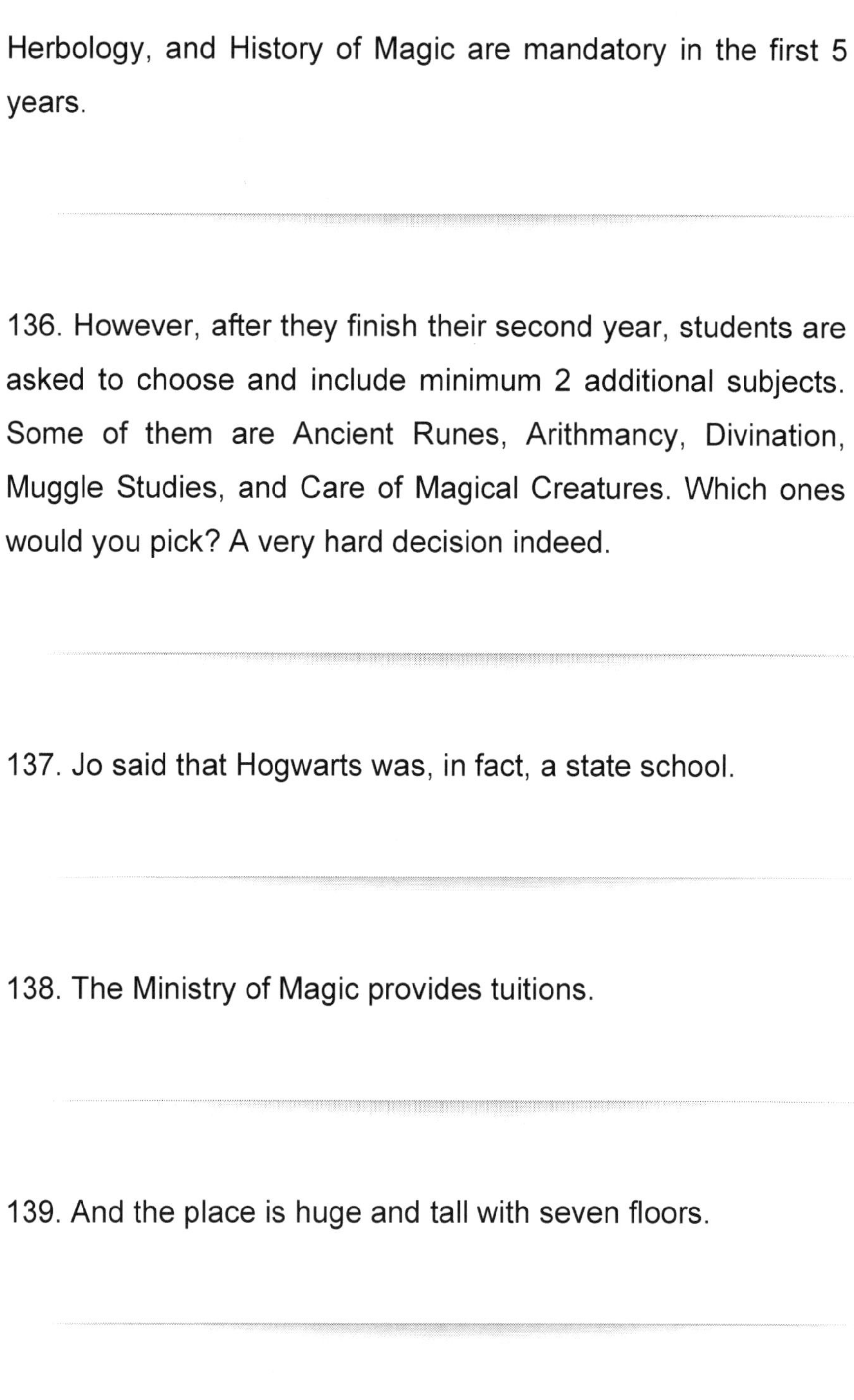

Herbology, and History of Magic are mandatory in the first 5 years.

136. However, after they finish their second year, students are asked to choose and include minimum 2 additional subjects. Some of them are Ancient Runes, Arithmancy, Divination, Muggle Studies, and Care of Magical Creatures. Which ones would you pick? A very hard decision indeed.

137. Jo said that Hogwarts was, in fact, a state school.

138. The Ministry of Magic provides tuitions.

139. And the place is huge and tall with seven floors.

140. It's funny how the official song of the school is sung only once in the first book and in the fourth movie when Hagrid and Hermione sing parts of it.

---

141. Just two Headmasters of Hogwarts have acquired this title multiple times. They are Minerva McGonagall and Albus Dumbledore.

---

142. In an interview, Rowling revealed that at any time there are around one thousand students at Hogwarts.

---

143. Hogwarts got its name thanks to Rowena Ravenclaw. Or that's how it's believed.

---

144. Apparently, she dreamed that a warty hog brought her to a lake.

145. The first Triwizard Tournament took place 300 years after Hogwarts was founded.

146. In case wizards and witches want to apparate or disapparate in and out of Hogwarts, they can’t possibly do that.

147. The only wizard capable of apparating and disapparating in and out of Hogwarts is no other than Albus Dumbledore.

148. Muggle technology like cell phones and Wi-Fi doesn’t work on Hogwarts grounds. Sorry!

149. The castle itself has a way of dealing with boys that sneak into the girls' dormitories. The stairs turn into slides. So, be careful!

---

150. The house elves work in Hogwarts's kitchens to produce food for the feasts.

---

151. They were brought to the school by Helga Hufflepuff, who wanted to find them refuge.

---

152. Hogwarts Grounds didn't have the Whomping Willow since forever. It was put by Dumbledore during the time Remus Lupin studied there to give him a place where he could go when changing into a werewolf.

---

153. There's a fancy frog choir at Hogwarts. It's summoned on special occasions to perform.

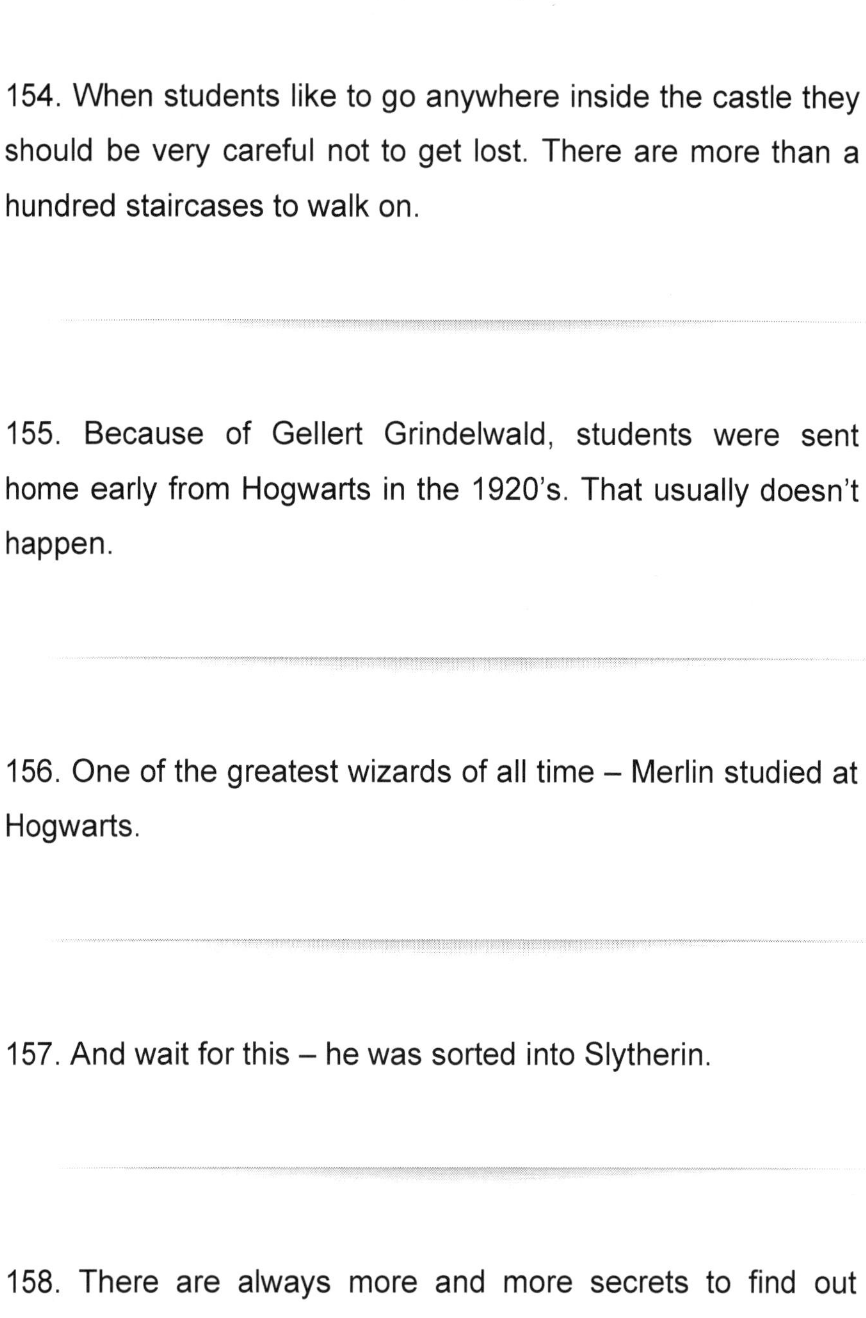

154. When students like to go anywhere inside the castle they should be very careful not to get lost. There are more than a hundred staircases to walk on.

155. Because of Gellert Grindelwald, students were sent home early from Hogwarts in the 1920's. That usually doesn't happen.

156. One of the greatest wizards of all time – Merlin studied at Hogwarts.

157. And wait for this – he was sorted into Slytherin.

158. There are always more and more secrets to find out about Hogwarts. No one knows them all.

159. After the catastrophic Battle of Hogwarts, the building started regenerating itself.

160. Naughty students should fear both their professors and Prefects. Why? Because Prefects are allowed to take points from the houses, too. Uh oh!

161. If it takes a student 5+ minutes to get sorted, he or she will be called 'Hatstall'.

162. You surely know that the Dementors can be chased away with the spell 'Expecto Patronum'. And this is so accurate since in Latin this can literally be translated to 'I await a guardian'.

163. The word 'Quidditch' took a lot of effort to invent. Jo Rowling wrote stunning 5 pages with words starting with the letter 'q' before finally making the decision.

---

164. In the books, the name 'Harry Potter' appears 18,956 times.

---

165. Petunia Dursley met Snape at one point.

---

166. In the third book, on Christmas, Trelawney doesn't want to sit on a table with twelve other people already seated. This is because she would be the thirteenth occupant of a seat and the one that stands up first would die.

---

167. Wizards can access Diagon Alley through the Leaky Cauldron from the Muggle side of London.

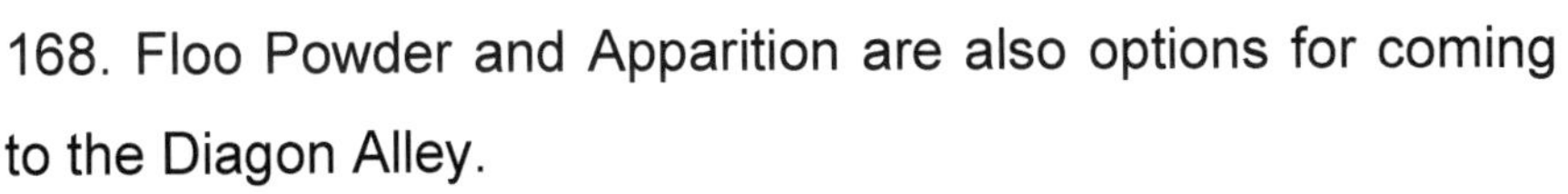

168. Floo Powder and Apparition are also options for coming to the Diagon Alley.

169. If pronounced wrong aka 'diagonally' the Floo powder brings people to a fireplace in Knockturn Alley, which is a darker place.

170. Both Diagon Alley and Knockturn Alley have very narrow streets, making them exclusively pedestrian places. No cars or other means of traffic are allowed.

171. There's a shop in Los Angeles called Whimsic Alley. It's a remake of the wizarding Diagon Alley.

FACTS ABOUT THE AUTHOR

Often called 'The Queen' by her most loyal fans, J.K. Rowling changed the childhoods and lives of millions of fans from all over the globe. Let's look deeper into the facts about Harry Potter's creator...

172. J.K. Rowling's real name is Joanne Rowling.

173. She added her grandmother's name 'Kathleen' and thus her publishing name was created.

174. One of her favorite chapters in the whole series is 'The Mirror of Erised' from *Harry Potter and the Philosopher's Stone*.

175. Dementors represent Rowling's depression.

---

176. Jo's mother died from multiple sclerosis.

---

177. So, death is one of the main themes in Harry Potter.

---

178. She has donated millions to the cause of finding a cure for multiple sclerosis.

---

179. Because of that, from a billionaire, she is now a millionaire.

---

180. Rowling told Oprah that if it weren't for her mother's death, the Harry Potter books probably wouldn't have existed.

181. When asked what she would teach and work in the wizarding world, Jo Rowling said she would want to teach Charms. Her job would be writing spell books, which we're totally down with!

182. J.K. Rowling is the founder of Lumos. That's a non-profit organization that wants to end institutionalization of children around the world.

183. She shares her birthday with Harry – they're both born on 31st July only in different years.

184. Jo was born in 1966.

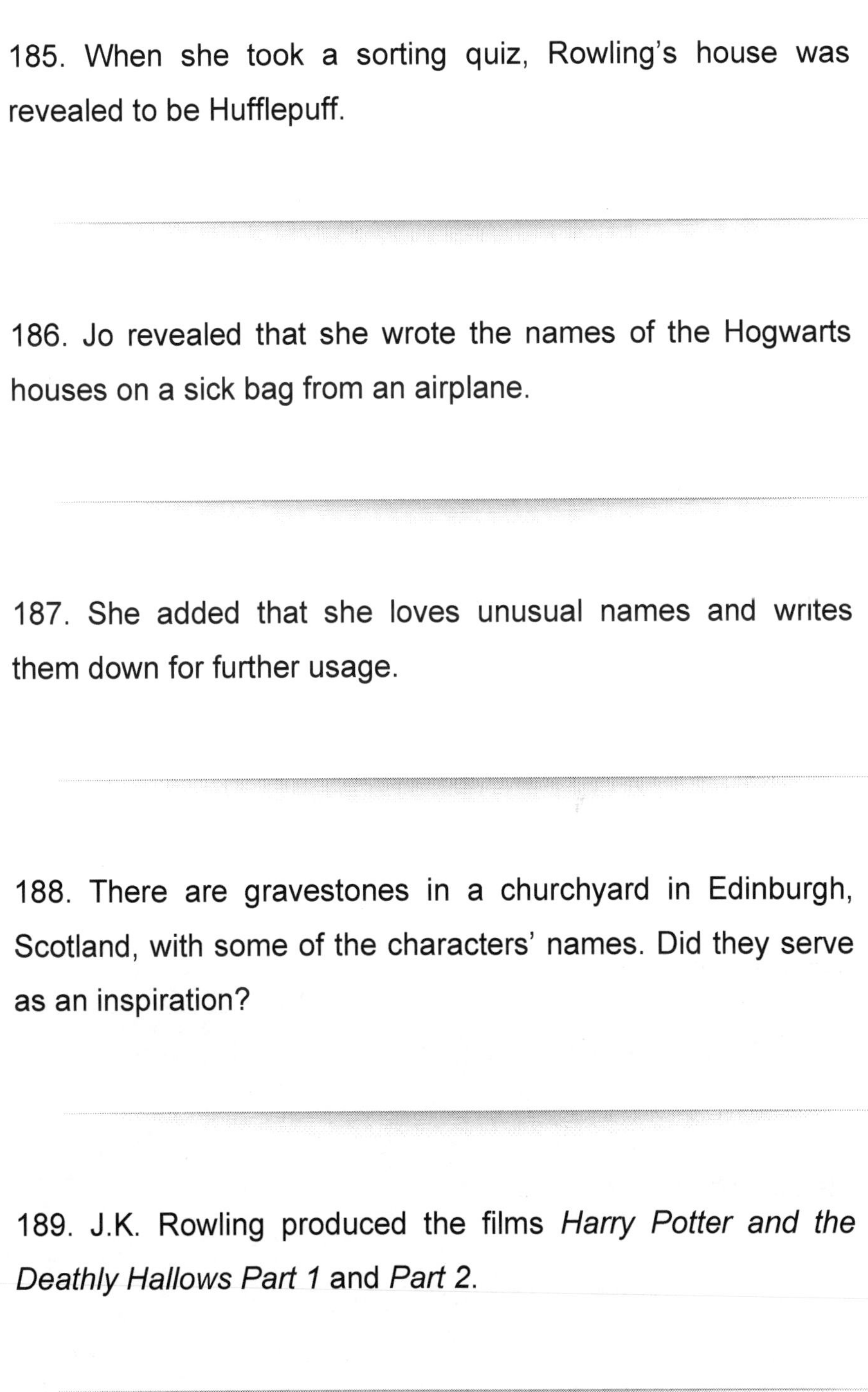

185. When she took a sorting quiz, Rowling's house was revealed to be Hufflepuff.

186. Jo revealed that she wrote the names of the Hogwarts houses on a sick bag from an airplane.

187. She added that she loves unusual names and writes them down for further usage.

188. There are gravestones in a churchyard in Edinburgh, Scotland, with some of the characters' names. Did they serve as an inspiration?

189. J.K. Rowling produced the films *Harry Potter and the Deathly Hallows Part 1* and *Part 2*.

190. After writing the Harry Potter series, she wrote her first books aimed at adults – the thriller named The Casual Vacancy which was then turned into a TV mini-series.

---

191. She published the *Cormoran Strike* detective book series under a pseudonym – Robert Galbraith.

---

192. J.K. Rowling decided that she couldn't leave the world for long (and so can't we). That's why she started developing spin-off movies set in the Harry Potter universe.

---

193. The title of the project is called *Fantastic Beasts*, which is loosely based on the textbook that exists in Hogwarts written by Newt Scamander.

---

194. The first of the Fantastic Beasts movies is called *Fantastic Beasts and Where to Find Them* starring Eddie Redmayne as the magizoologist Scamander.

195. Rowling wrote the screenplay for the movie, which was released in November 2016.

196. Rowling is set to write the screenplays for the rest of the planned Fantastic Beasts movies. And we couldn't be happier! Weee!

197. The second of the movies is called *Fantastic Beasts: The Crimes of Grindelwald* and is expected to hit theatres in November 2018.

198. If she could take a Polyjuice Potion, Jo said that she would transform herself into PM Tony Blair.

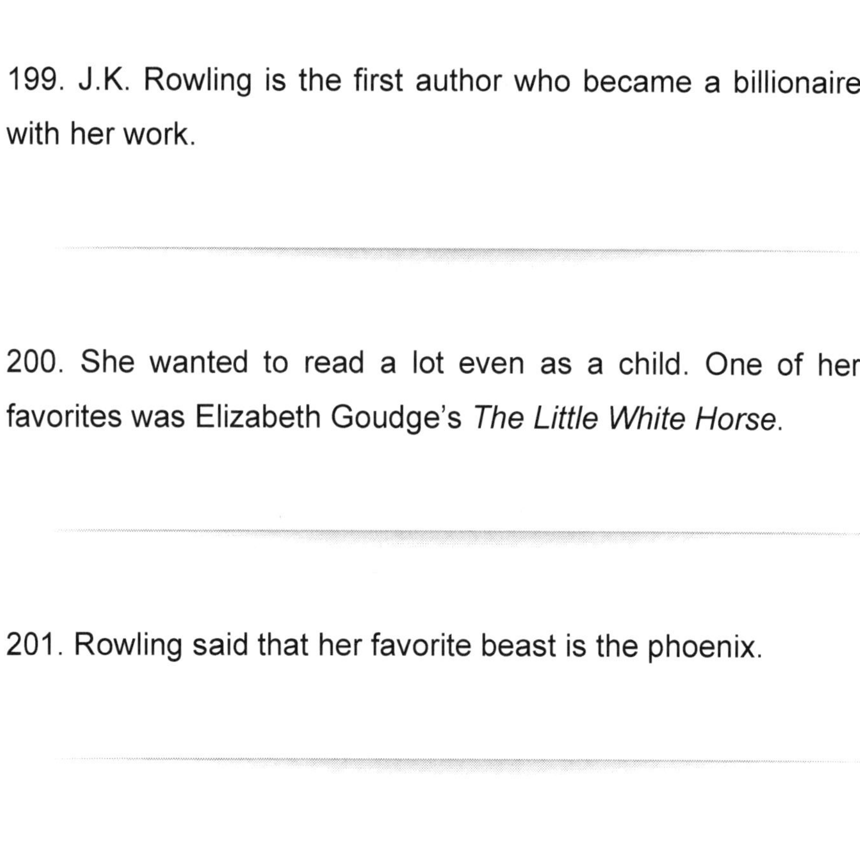

199. J.K. Rowling is the first author who became a billionaire with her work.

200. She wanted to read a lot even as a child. One of her favorites was Elizabeth Goudge's *The Little White Horse*.

201. Rowling said that her favorite beast is the phoenix.

202. The movie *Magic Beyond Words: The J.K. Rowling Story* is a biography movie depicting Jo Rowling's life, which was released in 2011. However, the author, herself, didn't support nor authorize it.

203. J.K. Rowling recently joined Twitter where she constantly shares her opinions and new information about Harry Potter and the growing universe.

204. Jo revealed to Daniel Radcliffe that she always knew how she was going to end the series. She had the vision of Hagrid carrying Harry in the Battle of Hogwarts since the beginning and that stuck with her through the entire series.

205. *Culpeper's Complete Herbal* by Nicholas Culpeper served as an inspiration for a lot of the plants Jo wrote about in the Harry Potter books.

206. She is a planner, so she had detailed outlines for the books and the story.

207. Jo Rowling admitted that she had always been afraid of the question "What is Dumbledore's wand made of?" Because it would become a big thing later on in the series and her answer might have set off some alarms.

---

208. When asked about her favorite chapter that she had to write in *Harry Potter and the Deathly Hallows*, she answered that it's the thirty-fourth chapter called 'The Forest Again'.

---

209. Rowling thinks that the muggle song that would be played on Dumbledore's funeral is 'My Way' by Frank Sinatra.

---

210. The student Natalie McDonald, who is mentioned in the fourth book, is a real person.

---

211. The girl was dying of leukemia and she wrote to Rowling asking her what will happen in the fifth book because she wasn't sure she was going to live to find out.

---

212. Jo wrote to her, but the girl sadly passed away before she got the email. In her honor, the author dedicated the character of Natalie – a brave Gryffindor.

---

213. Have you heard there is a documentary about Jo Rowling? It's called *J.K. Rowling: A Year in the Life* and follows the year when she completes the writing of the last Harry Potter book.

---

214. The most liked quote by J.K. Rowling on her Goodreads profile is, "If you want to know what a man's like, take a good look at how he treats his inferiors, not his equals."

---

215. Joanne Rowling was born in Bristol.

---

216. She spent her childhood in Gloucestershire in England, and in Gwent, Wales.

---

217. She became the writer of her first book when she was only six years old. The book had the title ‘Rabbit’.

---

218. Her biggest support was her sister Dianne.

---

219. She was the one, who read *Harry Potter and the Philosopher’s Stone* first.

---

220. Dr. Neill Murray is Jo’s husband. They’ve been married since 2001.

221. They have two children, a son Davis and daughter Mackenzie.

222. The four of them live in Edinburgh now.

223. Joanne has a daughter from her previous short marriage called Jessica.

224. She was writing Harry Potter and the Philosopher's Stone at a café in Edinburgh called Elephant House.

225. In her honor there are napkins dedicated to the series and the bathroom wall is full of messages or quotes people write while visiting the café. This is so cool!

226. Jo recently received The Royal Companion of Honor Award. Prince William gave it to her.

227. Rowling taught English in Portugal.

228. That's where she met her first husband Jorge Arantes.

229. Their marriage was very brief and lasted only three years.

230. Jo got her first daughter from that marriage.

231. After the divorce, she came back to England and lived as a single mum. Her only income was from social services.

232. She bought her dress for the wedding with Neil disguised so that no one recognized her. That's the high price of fame.

233. Rowling gave a commencement speech at the university Harvard in 2008.

234. She later published it as a self-improvement guide in 2015 with the title '*Very Good Lives: The Fringe Benefits of Failure and the Importance of Imagination*'.

235. All proceeds from this guide go to Lumos, her non-profit organization. Way to go, Jo!

236. She always loved the name Harry and that's why she gave it to her hero. She said that if her first daughter was born a boy she would have given him the name Harry.

HARRY POTTER FACTS ABOUT THE CHARACTERS

We see a plethora of wonderful characters in this rich wizarding world. From wizards and witches to trolls, fantastic beasts, giants, and elves, here are some facts about the characters…

237. Voldemort's name, in fact, means 'Flight of Death' in French. If that's not spooky, I don't know what is.

---

238. To the surprise of many, the ‘t’ in Voldemort is silent.

239. Earlier in the writing process, Draco Malfoy was given a slightly different last name. Some of Rowling’s choices were Smart, Spungen, and Spinks before she eventually settled on Malfoy.

240. The famous jokers Fred and George Weasley celebrate their birthday on April Fool’s Day (1st April). So accurate if you ask me.

241. These guys have also thrown a snowball at Voldemort once. Actually, they threw it at Professor Quirrell, but it hit the back of his head where Voldemort was living in the first book.

242. Did you know that Albus Dumbledore, Hogwarts's Headmaster, belonged to the house Gryffindor? And to show his pride he has a Griffin knocker on his office's door.

---

243. Dumbledore's full name is Albus Percival Wulfric Brian Dumbledore.

---

244. Dumbledore's name means 'Bumblebee' in Old English because the author imagined him humming to himself.

---

245. Before he was the headmaster of Hogwarts, Dumbledore taught Transfiguration and was even the Head of the Department. A guy with a real talent and potential!

---

246. Aberforth, who is Dumbledore's brother, works as a barman at the Hog's Head in the village Hogsmeade.

247. The famous alchemist Nicholas Flamel actually existed! And he was really associated with alchemy and the Philosopher's Stone.

248. After the books were published, J.K. Rowling announced that Dumbledore is gay.

249. Rubeus Hagrid is half-giant and half-human.

250. The character Hermione Granger is resembling J.K. Rowling.

251. Hermione even has a fashion line for house elves.

252. And she was the leader of S.P.E.W (Society for the Promotion of Elfish Welfare), which purpose was to free all house elves.

253. Hermione's career after Hogwarts began at the Department for the Regulation and Control of Magical Creatures at the Ministry of Magic where she continued her fight for the freedom of elves.

254. In the play *Harry Potter and the Cursed Child*, Hermione is the Minister of Magic.

255. Her Patronus is an otter.

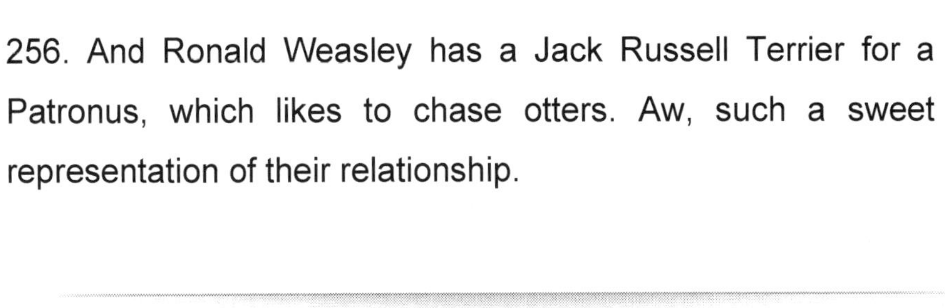

256. And Ronald Weasley has a Jack Russell Terrier for a Patronus, which likes to chase otters. Aw, such a sweet representation of their relationship.

---

257. Remember the wicked Knight Bus? Well, its conductor and driver got their names from Jo Rowling's grandfathers Stanley and Ernie.

---

258. Know Peeves the Poltergeist? If you've read the books you surely do as it can be found in all books and in none of the films.

---

259. The poltergeist Peeves causes mayhem and troubles to Hogwarts students.

---

260. Hermione Granger almost had a sister. Yeah, J.K. Rowling herself revealed in an interview that she had this in

mind, but since this character didn't appear in the first books, it was too late to introduce her later and she let it slide. Such a pity!

---

261. And wait till you hear this! The Chosen One could have easily been Neville Longbottom since he and Harry share Sybill Trelawney's prophecy and were born at the end of July.

---

262. Neville Longbottom ended up marrying Hannah Abbott after the Battle of Hogwarts.

---

263. Minerva McGonagall was an excellent Quidditch player while studying at Hogwarts. She was forced to quit because of a serious injury, though.

---

264. After she successfully completed her studies she met Dougal McGregor and fell madly in love with him.

265. Dougal McGregor was a Muggle.

266. Eventually, he asked her to marry him, but she refused out of fear that she would break the International Statute of Secrecy, which would cost her the dream job at the Ministry.

267. Minerva returned to London but resented her life. It was then that she joined Hogwarts this time as a teacher.

268. Minerva started teaching Transfiguration, which was one of the subjects she was really good at while studying.

269. Then, she married Elphinstone Urquart, her former boss at the Ministry.

---

270. He popped the question multiple times before she said 'yes'.

---

271. Unfortunately, venomous tentacula bit Elphinstone and he died unexpectedly leaving her a widow after only 3 years of marriage.

---

272. Minerva always stuck to her maiden surname, McGonagall.

---

273. After finishing her studies, Luna Lovegood ended up marrying Rolf Scamander.

---

274. He's the grandson of Newt Scamander, the hero of the new movie *Fantastic Beasts and Where to Find Them*.

275. She met Rolf while working as a naturalist.

276. And they have Lysander and Lorcan, who are their twin sons.

277. He can't get cooler than this. Albus Dumbledore has a scar showing the London Underground Map on his left knee.

278. Dumbledore's boggart is the corpse of his sister Ariana.

279. Remus Lupin has a wolf for his Patronus due to the fact that he despises all things connected to wolves.

280. His wife, Nymphadora Tonks originally had a Patronus in the form of a jackrabbit, but later on, it transformed into a wolf. That's what true love is about.

---

281. Lupin became a werewolf because of the revenge of Greyback, the werewolf.

---

282. Apparently, Remus's father, Lyall Lupin, insulted werewolves in front of Greyback and he decided to make his son one.

---

283. Can you believe that Voldemort was 71 when he lost his life in the Battle of Hogwarts? I didn't believe it at first either.

---

284. Speaking of You-Know-Who, he wasn't the first one to make Horcruxes. Herpo the Foul, a dark Greek wizard did it before him.

285. He bred a Basilisk first, as well.

286. Dumbledore shares Jo Rowling's love for sherbet lemons. Wizards have great taste!

287. One of the alternatives for the name Dolores Umbridge early on in the process was Elvira Umbridge.

288. Rowling said that Hermione should have married Harry instead of Ron. She and Ron would probably end in a couple's therapy, she added.

289. Have you wondered what's the inspiration behind the character Moaning Myrtle? The creator of the Harry Potter universe shared that she is based on girls who can be heard

crying in bathrooms at parties that she attended when she was young.

---

290. Our beloved trio – Harry, Ron, and Hermione – all have chocolate frog cards in the wizarding world.

---

291. The three of them unite Ollivander's three wand cores.

---

292. Harry Potter and Lord Voldemort are, in fact, distantly related through the Peverell blood that's flowing into the both of them.

---

293. Tom Marvolo Riddle aka Voldemort was conceived under the effects of a love potion.

---

294. Winky was a real star when she appeared in the Harry Potter book series. And all the fans rejoiced when Rowling spoke about her destiny since we left her – she is well, still in Hogwarts, and took part in the attack against the Death Eaters.

---

295. Harry Potter was born in Godric's Hollow.

---

296. Other famous wizards like Godric Gryffindor, himself, and the Dumbledores lived there, too.

---

297. Draco Malfoy was supposed to study at Durmstrang Institute.

---

298. Luckily, his mother interfered, because she didn't want him to be away from the family. He was eventually sent to Hogwarts.

---

299. Cho Chang wed a Muggle.

---

300. Severus Snape is largely inspired by J.K. Rowling's Chemistry teacher.

---

301. After they got married, Harry and Ginny named their children after people that meant to Harry a lot. Their children are called James Sirius, Albus Severus, and Lily Luna.

---

302. James Sirius, Harry's oldest son, started school in 2015 and was sorted into Gryffindor.

---

303. Albus Severus, however, was sorted into Slytherin.

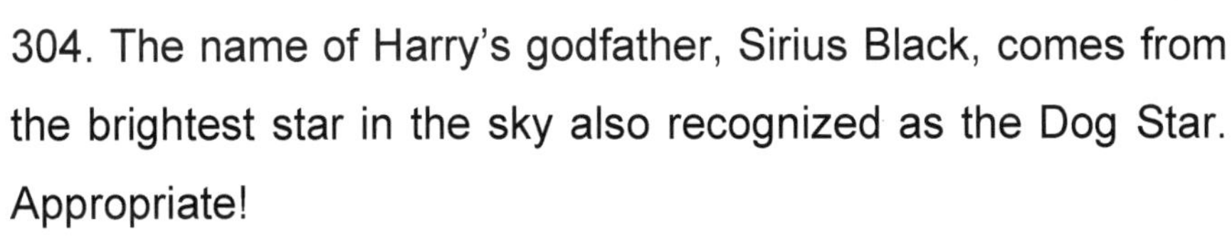

304. The name of Harry's godfather, Sirius Black, comes from the brightest star in the sky also recognized as the Dog Star. Appropriate!

305. Have you wondered what the middle names of your favorite trio are? The middle name of the Boy Who Lived is James, Hermione's middle name is Jane, and Ron's is Bilius.

306. Ron's actual first name is Ronald, but what is Ginny's? Her first full name is Ginevra.

307. Sirius Black's tattoos are inspired by the ones that Russian gang prisoners have. It means that that person is to be respected and feared.

308. Lily and James are real soulmates, even according to their patronuses. Lily's is a doe and James's is a stag. A perfect fit!

309. Harry's scar is shaped like a lightning bolt for no special reason. Rowling just thought it was cool and we can't agree more, can we?

310. Molly Weasley's favorite singer is Celestina Warbeck.

311. She danced with Arthur when she was 18 on Warbeck's song 'A Cauldron Full of Hot, Strong Love'.

312. After Fred died, George was unable to conjure a Patronus again.

313. Dumbledore was around 150 years old when he passed away.

---

314. After Remus Lupin died, he was rewarded with the Order of Merlin, First Class.

---

315. He was the first werewolf to receive the reward.

---

316. Ginny went on to become a professional Quidditch player after the Battle of Hogwarts ended. She joined the Holyhead Harpies.

---

317. But the birth of her son ended that career since she decided to spend more time with her family and became a sports journalist instead.

---

318. Petunia Dursley has always wanted to be a wizard.

---

319. In the past, wizards used to duel with swords.

---

320. Godric Gryffindor was very successful with that. That's where the Sword of Gryffindor comes in the picture.

---

321. James, Harry's eldest son, eventually stole the Marauder's Map from his father's desk. Like father like son!

---

322. Rowling nearly enriched the Weasley family with one more member - a cousin that was supposed to be in Slytherin. It would have been tough for him with a house full of Gryffindors.

---

323. Despite looking older, Severus Snape had only 38 years when he died. What? I was surprised, too.

324. Dobby, the house-elf, loves Harry unconditionally. There isn't a bigger proof of that than this. His first and last words are 'Harry Potter'.

325. Pansy Parkinson, the mischievous Slytherin girl, depicts the girl that teased Rowling at school.

326. She didn't wed Draco Malfoy because Jo hated her.

327. At first, Neville asked the Sorting Hat to put him in Hufflepuff.

328. Here's a devastating one. The twin brothers Fred and George Weasley had the chance to see each other as old people only when they made an incident with their names in the Goblet of Fire.

---

329. When the Horcrux inside Harry was destroyed by Voldemort, he could no longer speak Parseltongue.

---

330. Harry kept in touch with his cousin Dudley, even bringing his children to visit.

---

331. Severus Snape is a great Legilimens, meaning he can enter people's minds. That's how he knew about Harry's adventures at Hogwarts during the night.

FACTS ABOUT THE MOVIES

Hailed as some of the best movies ever made, the Harry Potter motion pictures have kept fans excited and wanting for more magic. With an all-star cast and breath-taking visual effects, it's impossible not to love them. So, here are the facts about the Harry Potter films…

332. The actress, Shirley Henderson, who portrays Moaning Myrtle was, in fact, 37 when she appeared in the movies, making her the oldest actress to play a student in the films.

---

333. Did you spot this in *Harry Potter and the Chamber of Secrets*? There's a picture of Gandalf the Grey (the well-known wizard from *The Lord of the Rings*) hanging in Dumbledore's office.

---

334. Alfonso Cuaron, who directed *Harry Potter and the Prisoner of Azkaban*, made the trio write an essay about their characters. Daniel Radcliffe wrote one page, Rupert Grint didn't write anything, and Emma Watson appeared with an essay of TEN pages! So like their characters!

---

335. The Great Hall's dining tables in *Harry Potter and the Philosopher's Stone* had real food on them.

---

336. More than 160 pairs of glasses were used by Daniel Radcliffe during all eight films.

---

337. He broke more than 80 wands on the set of the movies while utilizing them as drumsticks.

---

338. Wondering why Daniel Radcliffe doesn't have green eyes in the movies like Harry is supposed to have in the books? The actor had struggles with the contact lenses. Poor him!

---

339. Alan Rickman was chosen to play Severus Snape by J.K. Rowling, herself. What an honor!

---

340. He knew a lot of spoilers before everyone else. Rowling told him so many details so that he can get into the role of the strict professor.

---

341. All the child actors had to do their actual homework on set so that the school Hogwarts would be more real.

---

342. Several American actors were declined for roles in the Harry Potter movies including Robin Williams. The reason was that Rowling wanted only British or Irish actors aboard.

343. Are you a couch potato? Are you planning to spend your whole day in bed watching TV? If that's a yes, listen up! You'll need around 18 hours and a half to watch all Harry Potter films.

344. While she was filming *Harry Potter and the Half-Blood Prince*, Dame Maggie Smith was having therapies for battling her breast cancer.

345. And she finally defeated it like the real-life McGonagall she is!

346. Even though there are 7 books, there are 8 Harry Potter movies. Because of the length of the final book, it was decided to split the last book into 2 movies. Smart!

347. *Harry Potter and the Deathly Hallows Part 2* is officially the shortest-running film in the movie series lasting two hours and ten minutes.

---

348. Would you like to see Tom Felton as Harry or Ron? Well, he actually auditioned and read lines for those two roles before eventually getting Draco Malfoy.

---

349. The famous American director Steven Spielberg was attached to *Harry Potter and the Philosopher's Stone*, but after a creative conflict he dropped out.

---

350. He was replaced by Chris Columbus who helmed the first two Harry Potter movies.

---

351. When Steven Spielberg was interested in directing Harry Potter, he suggested Haley Joel Osment for the role of Harry.

352. The third film, *Harry Potter and the Prisoner of Azkaban*, was directed by Alfonso Cuaron, a then newbie in the business who would later go on and win an Academy Award.

353. Things changed again when Mike Newell sat in the director's chair for *Harry Potter and the Goblet of Fire*.

354. The fifth, sixth, seventh, and eighth installment of Harry's adventure on the big screen all had David Yates as the director.

355. Steve Kloves is the screenwriter of all Harry Potter movies except one – *Harry Potter and the Order of the Phoenix*.

356. The fifth Harry Potter film was written by Michael Goldenberg, known for penning *Peter Pan*, *Green Lantern*, *Contact*, and other films.

---

357. The London premiere of the last Harry Potter movie made history at Trafalgar Square with a huge number of visitors and fans. And a lot of tears if I may add.

---

358. Call it destiny or something else… the screenwriter of the first Harry Potter film – Steve Kloves – and the producer – David Heyman – went together to the theatre where they spotted the young Daniel Radcliffe with his family. They knew that he was the right choice.

---

359. Rupert Grint's audition is a story all to itself. He decided to be creative and made a rap video of himself about how he wanted to play Ron on-screen.

---

360. Emma Watson didn't want to audition for the role of Hermione Granger at first. But her teacher eventually persuaded her and she was the last girl that day to audition.

---

361. The young actress was given only 50 pounds pocket money a week by her parents until she turned eighteen.

---

362. The brooms which are used in the movies aren't regular brooms! The guys behind the scenes worked their movie magic to create them specifically for the actors to sit on them comfortably.

---

363. Rik Mayall, the renowned British comedian, was originally cast as Peeves, but then his scenes got cut.

---

364. Mandrakes, which appear in *Harry Potter and the Chamber of Secrets*, weren't computer generated.

365. Can you believe how many times the make-up team applied and reapplied Harry's lightning bolt onto Dan Radcliffe's forehead? 5800 times!

366. The actress who portrays Bellatrix Lestrange – Helena Bonham Carter – loved the fake teeth her character was having, so she kept them.

367. Believe it or not! Michael Jackson – the king of pop, himself – was once interested in doing a Harry Potter musical.

368. During the press junkets of the first movies, Emma Watson said that there's no chance she would kiss Daniel or Rupert. Oh, how wrong she was!

369. Rupert Grint, just like Ron, is afraid of spiders.

---

370. The first person to be cast in the first Harry Potter movie was Robbie Coltrane for the role of Rubeus Hagrid.

---

371. Hagrid's Hut was a real place, built just for the first film. Unfortunately, it was demolished.

---

372. Everyone loves Hedwig. The snowy-white owl was played by 7 owls throughout the film series.

---

373. The cat that played Mrs. Norris in *Harry Potter and the Philosopher's Stone* ran away from the set, causing a bit of trouble.

---

374. Luckily, it came back 2 days after that.

---

375. The flashback scenes in *Harry Potter and the Philosopher's Stone* when Voldemort kills Lily and James were written by none other than J.K. Rowling.

---

376. Hermione has pretty big teeth in the books and they wanted the same thing with Emma Watson. But, she had a lot of trouble speaking, so the fake buck teeth were out.

---

377. For the purposes of the second film, Daniel Radcliffe had to shave off one of his legs. The scene in question is the one when he shows he's missing a sock.

---

378. An outbreak of lice occurred on the filming between the young actors.

379. During the shooting of *Prisoner of Azkaban*, Tom Felton's Hogwarts robes pockets were sewn shut to prevent him from taking any food. Sneaky Draco!

380. The scenes on Number 4 Privet Drive were shot in an actual house. But it wasn't available for reshoots, so they had to build an exact replica.

381. All the acceptance letters Harry got were handwritten not once, but TWICE! The first ones were too heavy for the owls to carry, so they had to handwrite them again.

382. The owls have been taught how to carry them for six months.

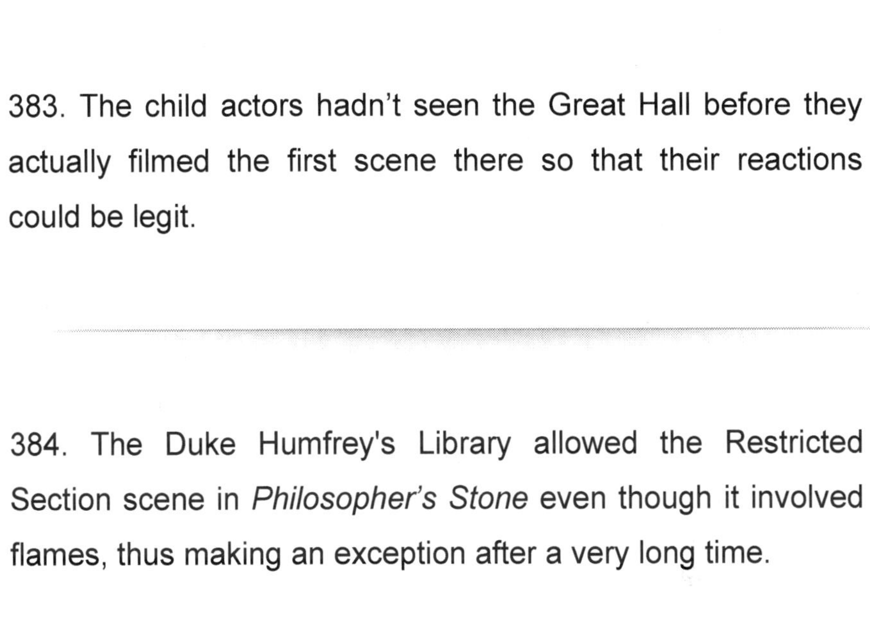

383. The child actors hadn't seen the Great Hall before they actually filmed the first scene there so that their reactions could be legit.

384. The Duke Humfrey's Library allowed the Restricted Section scene in *Philosopher's Stone* even though it involved flames, thus making an exception after a very long time.

385. J.K. Rowling was offered to play Lily Potter, Harry's mum, in the Mirror of Erised scene. After turning it down, the role was given to Geraldine Somerville.

386. Fourteen Ford Anglias were destroyed while shooting The Whomping Willow scene in *Chamber of Secrets*!

387. Gilderoy Lockhart would have easily gotten Hugh Grant's face! He had scheduling conflicts, so he dropped out.

388. Richard Harris, who played Dumbledore in the first and second films, sadly died and the Headmaster had to be recast.

389. Michael Gambon stepped into his shoes, playing Dumbledore from the third movie onward.

390. The trio got rid of their school uniforms (at least in several scenes) for the first time in the third movie. The director thought that it would show off their individuality.

391. During the Yule Ball scene, Daniel Radcliffe is mostly shot from the waist up because he didn't have much time to practice his dancing due to filming.

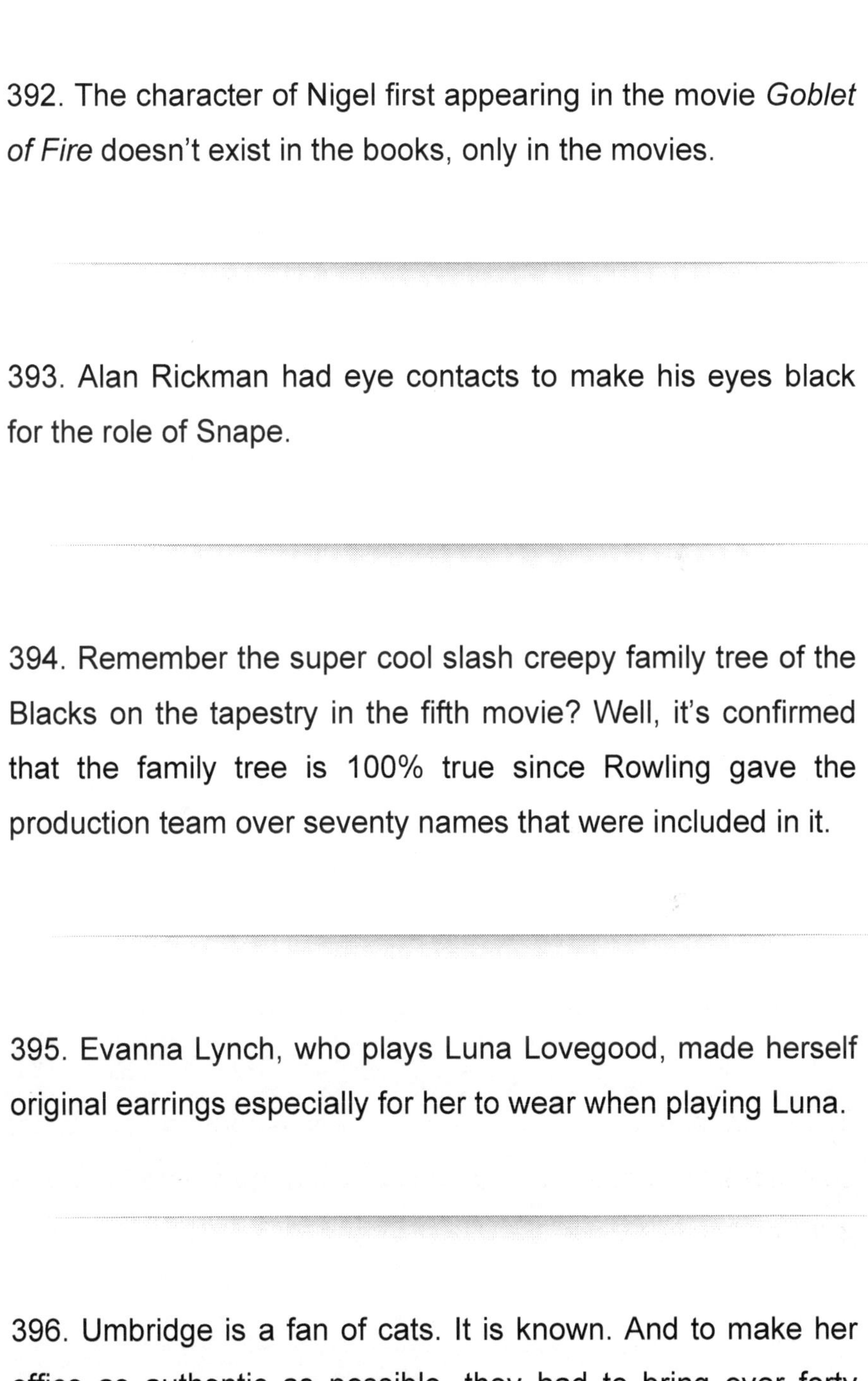

392. The character of Nigel first appearing in the movie *Goblet of Fire* doesn't exist in the books, only in the movies.

393. Alan Rickman had eye contacts to make his eyes black for the role of Snape.

394. Remember the super cool slash creepy family tree of the Blacks on the tapestry in the fifth movie? Well, it's confirmed that the family tree is 100% true since Rowling gave the production team over seventy names that were included in it.

395. Evanna Lynch, who plays Luna Lovegood, made herself original earrings especially for her to wear when playing Luna.

396. Umbridge is a fan of cats. It is known. And to make her office as authentic as possible, they had to bring over forty small cats for a special photo shoot.

397. Tonks's hair is purple in the movies, whereas her book-version has a pink one.

398. The young Tom Riddle that appears in the flashback scene in *Half-Blood Prince* is actually related to Ralph Fiennes who plays the grown-up Voldemort!

399. The actors who portray Mad-Eye Moody and Bill Weasley are father and son.

400. The scene of the Seven Harrys is one of the most complex and hardest-to-pull-off scenes in the whole franchise with over ninety takes.

401. The Voldemort-Draco hug in the last movie wasn't planned. It was improvised by Fiennes, himself.

---

402. The famous composer, John Williams, composed Hedwig's Theme which is the theme song of the whole Harry Potter film series.

---

403. He is the guy behind the soundtracks of some of the movies as well.

---

404. Gary Oldman (Sirius) bought Daniel Radcliffe (Harry) a bass guitar because he knew Dan loved music. Aww, like a real godfather!

---

405. In one of the takes for the scene when Hermione climbs down the stairs before the Yule Ball, Emma Watson tripped and fell.

406. In *Half-Blood Prince* when Ron is on the ground and foam is coming out of his mouth, the foam was, in fact, made of egg white. Ew! Ew! Ew!

407. *Harry Potter and the Deathly Hallows Part 1* is the first and only movie where the plot doesn't revolve around Hogwarts and trio is away from school for the first time.

408. Forty props were made of the Slytherin locket because Harry and Ron had to destroy it over and over again until the perfect shot was made.

409. M. Night Shyamalan was once interested to direct a Harry Potter movie.

410. Tom Felton brought his girlfriend to play Draco's wife in the epilogue.

---

411. Up until his twenty-first year, Daniel Radcliffe had earned more than 40 million pounds.

---

412. Oliver Phelps could do very few takes of the scene when Fred dies because seeing his brother acting dead was too emotionally exhausting for him.

---

413. We have to thank Richard Harris's granddaughter because she is the reason why he accepted the role of Dumbledore.

---

414. Daniel Radcliffe (Harry) and Dame Maggie Smith (Professor McGonagall) were in a movie together before Harry Potter. It's called *David Copperfield.*

415. BBC filmed in 2001 a Christmas special called *Harry Potter and Me*.

416. It's, in fact, an interview with the author in which she gave insight into her world.

417. Another such famous interview happened in 2012 called *Harry Potter: Beyond the Page*.

418. *The Queen's Handbag* is a skit that lasts three minutes and was made as a celebration of the Queen's 80th birthday.

419. It was filmed during the production of the fifth film and stars Daniel Radcliffe, Rupert Grint, Emma Watson, and Matthew Lewis played their respective roles.

420. Evanna Lynch, the actress who portrays Luna Lovegood, was having a hard time with her eating disorder even before she was a part of the movies.

421. She decided to write to Rowling about how her books empowered her to fight her illness and the author wrote back. So they became pen pals even before Evanna brought Luna to the big screen.

422. Tom Felton forgot his line and improvised the sentence that'll become one of his funniest ones 'I didn't know you could read' referring to Goyle aka Harry who was transformed in him with the Polyjuice Potion.

423. The windows of the shops in Diagon Alley had 20,000 goods and packages.

424. Ever considered Yellow Pages as useful? Well, it truly is as most of the shelves in Dumbledore's office were filled with Yellow Pages books wrapped as old books.

425. Some Hogwarts spots were filmed in the Oxford University.

426. All eight movies required more than 588 sets.

427. The doors at Gringotts were designed to truly work. It's amazing how much time the team spent on the details.

428. Only one real staircase was made for the films and the others were designed with the help of the visual effects.

429. The members of the cast and crew put themselves in the Hogwarts's portraits. For one, you can spot Stuart Craig up there. Such a great idea.

430. In the classroom with potions, there are more than a thousand bottles.

431. And the potions the actors drank were mostly filled with soup.

432. The potion jars, however, were full of dried herbs, leaves, and bones from a butcher shop nearby.

433. For the unique clock of the Weasleys, the filmmakers used scissors as the hands.

434. For the movies, over 60 goblin types were created.

435. A special model of the Hogwarts castle was made for filming the exterior scenes.

436. A team of forty people made it in seven months.

437. It took three months to craft the bridge alone.

438. And they used salt for snow, but quickly wiped it away to prevent disintegration.

439. The telescope in Dumbledore's office was one of the most expensive objects on the set.

---

440. There was a specific design for every Death Eater mask.

---

441. The Howler was inspired by origami. It doesn't look so scary now, does it?

---

442. The crazily fast Knight Bus was truly created by merging three older double-decker London buses.

---

443. Because of the scenes with the Knight Bus, certain streets in London were closed eight weeks.

---

444. The only costume that remained the same during the filming of all movies was Snape's.

445. Rupert Grint had the most awkward experience on set when he drew a not-so-nice picture of Alan Rickman, who has the role of Snape, and he was overlooking from behind. Oh, no!

446. The actor, who brought Harry to life – Daniel Radcliffe is a huge fan of the Simpsons.

447. He was even given the voice of Edward Cullen from Twilight in a Simpsons Halloween episode.

448. The real Draco aka Tom Felton never knew anything about the films he was going to play in. That's because he hasn't read any of the books before coming to the audition.

449. The eight Harry Potter all together have 12 Oscar nominations in total.

450. The duel between Snape and McGonagall in the last film was in one stage supposed to happen between Snape and Harry. But the idea was scrapped by the author, herself.

451. Whenever Voldemort and Bellatrix appear together, she is standing to his right. That's the position of the most reliable and loyal follower.

452. Every wand created for the movies was unique and there were no two exact-looking wands.

453. Most of the events in the final Potter movie happen during one day.

---

454. *Harry Potter and the Deathly Hallows Part 2* is the only movie in which we can see Hermione riding a broomstick. You go, girl!

---

455. When the last movie was released, it broke the record for biggest box office opening weekend.

---

456. When Emma Watson entered the set of Hermione's bedroom, she told the production team that more books were needed. They were happy to oblige.

---

457. Daniel Radcliffe's stunt double was seriously injured on the set of the seventh movie.

458. The exterior of the manor of the Malfoys is, in fact, Hardwick Hall.

459. Rhys Ifans, who plays Luna's father, said that he has never read the books. However, he decided to take on the role, because he loved the idea of working with a cast composed of such famous stars.

460. Alexandre Desplat was in charge of the soundtracks of the last two Harry Potter movies.

461. Nicholas Hooper is the film composer of the soundtracks of the fifth and sixth movie.

462. Patrick Doyle composed the soundtrack of *Harry Potter and the Goblet of Fire*.

463. Chris Columbus has a figurine of Dobby in his office.

FACTS ABOUT THE THEME PARKS AND MERCHANDISE

Finally, the official theme parks and the Harry Potter merchandise and items are a gigantic part of the whole global phenomenon. These are some of the most interesting facts about the Harry Potter theme parks and products...

464. The name of the Harry Potter fans is Potterheads.

465. May 2nd, the day when the Battle of Hogwarts occurred is considered as International Harry Potter Day by fans. So make sure you mark your calendars and raise your wands!

466. The first Harry Potter amusement park was constructed in 2001.

467. It was called Harry Potter Movie Magic Experience at Warner Bros. Movie World and was set in Australia.

468. It represented a walkthrough, tiny space that featured some of the well-known locations from the first movies. Sadly, it was removed.

469. The first big theme park with its own official opening in 2010 was branded as The Wizarding World of Harry Potter, located at the Universal Orlando Resort.

---

470. The Wizarding World of Harry Potter theme park cost 200 million dollars to make.

---

471. Some of the most visited attractions there include Flight of the Hippogriff, the Forbidden Journey, Dragon Challenge, Hogwarts Express, and many, many more. It's on the top of our places-to-visit list.

---

472. Daniel Radcliffe, Emma Watson, Rupert Grint joined by other fellow co-stars even filmed exclusive sequences which appear as holograms at the park.

---

473. Other such theme parks followed at the Universal Studios Hollywood and Universal Studios Japan.

---

474. Before getting a job at the Wizarding World of Harry Potter, all staff members are required to pass a test about their Harry Potter knowledge. Think you can pass it?

---

475. The British accent can be heard all around the Harry Potter parks as a lot of Britons are regularly hired to work there.

---

476. Now, these are some excellent news. You can truly buy yourself a magical wand from Ollivander's Wand Shop.

---

477. There's a whole ceremony before the wand 'chooses you'. This involves standing on a plaque and uttering different spells that are given. Each of them provokes a specific

outcome and the right one will make the light appear above you. Just like Harry!

---

478. Inside the Wizarding World, visitors have the opportunity to ride the Hogwarts Express between King's Cross and Hogsmeade Station.

---

479. The first year after this world was open to the public a stellar number of 5 million visitors rode the Hogwarts Express. Just wow!

---

480. In Diagon Alley in the parks, there's a dragon that breathes fire. Like literally!

---

481. Ever dreamed of having a deep conversation with a goblin? Well, this dream will become reality in the Wizarding World of Harry Potter as once you enter Gringotts Bank, an

animated goblin will appear. You can then ask him some basic questions and see how he replies.

---

482. There's an option to exchange your Muggle money with Gringotts coins and buy things with them in the park.

---

483. You can buy original Butterbeer in the real world.

---

484. While walking down the streets in the park, visitors get the unique opportunity to see Beauxbatons and Durmstrang students perform a special act.

---

485. Most of the scenes in the Harry Potter movies were shot in Leavesden Studios in Watford.

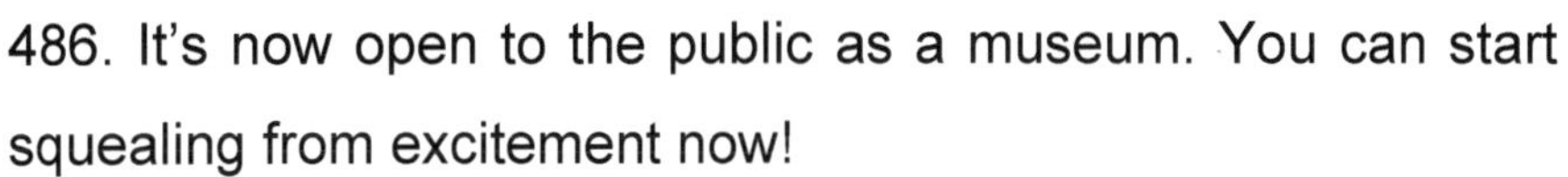

486. It's now open to the public as a museum. You can start squealing from excitement now!

487. And inside visitors get to walk on the most notable sets where the actors filmed the iconic scenes. Of course, Hogwarts's Great Hall is one of them.

488. Harry Potter: The Exhibition is an exhibit show that travels all over the world, visiting North America, Europe, Asia, Australia, and so on.

489. The exhibition features more than 200 props and replica items from Harry Potter including the costumes, the Horcruxes, the gigantic pieces from the Wizard Chess and many more.

490. Are you a fan of playing video games? Do you love Harry Potter more than anything? We have the perfect combo! There are eight Harry Potter video games made by EA Games. And you should be definitely checking them out if you haven't already.

---

491. The Harry Potter series got the Funko Pop treatment! Now you can find the cute small Funko Pop figurines of all your favorite Harry Potter characters almost everywhere.

---

492. Besides that, you can buy special Harry Potter LEGO figures and scenes.

---

493. There are also video games which are based on the Harry Potter LEGO toys.

---

494. Quidditch fans, listen up! Harry Potter: Quidditch World Cup is an action video game where you get the chance to play Quidditch both at Hogwarts and at the World Cup.

---

495. In 2005, the sold Harry Potter merchandise went above one billion pounds.

---

496. Can't get enough of Hogwarts? *Harry Potter: A Pop-Up Book* features amazing pop-up versions of important locations and events as well as some other extras.

---

497. *Harry Potter Film Wizardry* is another terrific book that gives the fans some unique information you've never heard before. Plus, there are some extras and prop replicas that come with it.

---

498. *Harry Potter Page to Screen: The Complete Filmmaking Journey* is also a wonderful book that details all the behind-the-scenes secrets and magic in around 600 pages.

---

499. Asher Silva Vargas, a Mexican lawyer, holds the Guinness World Record for his biggest collection of Harry Potter items and merchandise in the world. His collection has 3,000 pieces.

---

500. Another Guinness World Record for Harry Potter. 676 Harrys, to be precise. In 2017, 676 people dressed as Harry Potter gathered together and set this brilliant record in celebration of the twentieth anniversary of the first book. Hats off to you, guys!

How did you like these facts? Do you have some other fact you may want to add? If you want to share something, email me: info@donaldshaw.org – I promise to respond to all your emails!

FREE BOOKS FROM DONALD SHAW

Thanks for reading my book! I hope it was fun!

For a limited time, my husband, and a well-known comic and author, Donald Shaw, is giving away his HUMOR LIBRARY for FREE. You can see three books from the library pictured above. No strings attached.

Please, follow the link: **http://donaldshaw.org/facts/**

YOUR REVIEWS AND MORE FUN BOOKS

Your reviews are extremely important!

If you have enjoyed this book, please consider leaving a short review on the book's **Amazon Page**. It will help the others to make an informed decision before buying my book.

Please, also check **my other books on Amazon**.

Made in the USA
San Bernardino, CA
01 December 2018